OCCUPYING
ALCATRAZ

NATIVE AMERICAN ACTIVISTS
DEMAND CHANGE

BY ALEXIS BURLING

CONTENT CONSULTANT
ROBERT WARRIOR
HALL DISTINGUISHED PROFESSOR OF AMERICAN
LITERATURE AND CULTURE
UNIVERSITY OF KANSAS

Essential Library

An Imprint of Abdo Publishing | abdopublishing.com

ABDOPUBLISHING.COM

Published by Abdo Publishing, a division of ABDO, PO Box 398166, Minneapolis, Minnesota 55439. Copyright © 2017 by Abdo Consulting Group, Inc. International copyrights reserved in all countries. No part of this book may be reproduced in any form without written permission from the publisher. Essential Library™ is a trademark and logo of Abdo Publishing.

Printed in the United States of America, North Mankato, Minnesota
102016
012017

**THIS BOOK CONTAINS
RECYCLED MATERIALS**

Cover Photo: Robert W. Klein/AP Images
Interior Photos: Ernest K. Bennett/AP Images, 4–5; AP Images, 11, 38–39, 53, 60–61, 68, 70; Sal Veder/AP Images, 13, 81; Hulton Archive/Getty Images, 14–15; Library of Congress/Corbis/VCG/Getty Images, 18; Library of Congress, 23; Frances Benjamin Johnston Collection/Library of Congress, 24; MPI/Getty Images, 26–27; EOH/AP Images, 30; Duane Howell/The Denver Post/Getty Images, 34; Ernst Haas/Getty Images, 36; iStockphoto, 42–43; Bill Beattie/AP Images, 46; Robert W. Klein/AP Images, 49, 50–51, 82; Dick Drew/AP Images, 65; BB/AP Images, 72–73; Bettmann/Getty Images, 75, 84–85; Jim Mone/AP Images, 90; Tom Lynn/AP Images, 93; Kara Andrade/AFP/Getty Images, 95; Shutterstock Images, 96

Editor: Arnold Ringstad
Series Designer: Maggie Villaume

PUBLISHER'S CATALOGING-IN-PUBLICATION DATA

Names: Burling, Alexis, author.
Title: Occupying Alcatraz: Native American activists demand change / by Alexis Burling.
Other titles: Native American activists demand change
Description: Minneapolis, MN : Abdo Publishing, 2017. | Series: Hidden heroes | Includes bibliographical references and index.
Identifiers: LCCN 2016945473 | ISBN 9781680783896 (lib. bdg.) | ISBN 9781680797428 (ebook)
Subjects: LCSH: Prisons--California--Alcatraz Island--Juvenile literature. | United States Penitentiary, Alcatraz Island, California--Juvenile literature. | Military prisons--United States--Juvenile literature. | Alcatraz Island (Calif.)--Juvenile literature.
Classification: DDC 365--dc23
LC record available at http://lccn.loc.gov/2016945473

CONTENTS

CHAPTER ONE

AN ATTEMPTED INVASION

Sunday, March 8, 1964, was no ordinary day. That afternoon, A. L. Aylworth noticed a strange commotion brewing by the waterfront on Alcatraz Island in San Francisco, California. Aylworth was the caretaker of the recently shuttered prison on Alcatraz. As he drove his rusty pickup truck toward the dock, he spied a crowd of approximately 40 Native Americans and several members of the media in boats by the shore.[1]

Not knowing their intentions, Aylworth approached the group and politely asked them to vacate the island. As he began to explain they were trespassing, Elliot Leighton, a lawyer from the American Indian Council,

Alcatraz, which sits in San Francisco Bay, was a federal prison from 1934 to 1963.

stepped forward. Leighton flipped open his briefcase, took out a stack of papers, and began reciting the Sioux Treaty of 1868 aloud:

> *And it is further stipulated that any male Indians, over eighteen years of age, of any band or tribe that is or who shall hereafter become a party to this treaty, who now is or shall hereafter become a resident or occupant of any reservation or territory not included in this tract of country designated . . . which is not mineral land, nor reserved by the United States for any special purpose other than Indian occupation . . . shall be entitled to receive from the United States a [right to the land].*[2]

When Leighton finished, Aylworth looked around at each member of the group. He grunted and scratched his head. Though the reference to the 1868 treaty was not a serious legal route to seizing the island, it was clear the protesters were serious about getting their message across. As if realizing that matters had gotten out of his control, Aylworth shrugged and said, "Well, I guess if you want it, you can have it."[3]

A Desire for Action

In the weeks and months leading up to that fateful March day, the Native American community in the San Francisco Bay Area had been searching for a way for their voices to be heard. Like many Native Americans throughout the country, they had become frustrated by their increasing lack of civil liberties and loss of control over their ancestors' land. For years they had been embroiled in ferocious legal battles in the courts and through the Indian Claims Commission (ICC) to receive monetary compensation for these losses. It was time to do something drastic—a protest that would force the government to act and bring about positive change for Native American people.

One group in particular, the San Francisco Sioux Club, had already been working on a plan. After the federal prison on Alcatraz Island closed in 1963, the US Justice Department declared the land

THE TREATY OF 1868

During the mid-1800s, the US government enacted a series of treaties that forced Native Americans to give up their land and move onto federally sanctioned reservations. In 1868, a council was held at Fort Laramie, in present-day Wyoming. The result of the meeting was a treaty with the Sioux, which entitled the tribe to land in the surrounding Black Hills.

But in 1874, General George A. Custer led an expedition into the Black Hills. What he and his men found there—gold—changed the situation dramatically. They immediately started encroaching on Sioux hunting territory to find more. The Sioux fought back. Two years later, the Sioux defeated Custer and his troops in a fierce battle at Little Bighorn River. In retaliation, the US government confiscated the land from the Sioux in 1877. The question of who actually owns the land—the government or the Sioux—is hotly disputed to this day.

INDIAN CLAIMS COMMISSION

The US Congress created the ICC on August 13, 1946, for the purpose of hearing and processing legal claims made by Native Americans against the United States. Most of these claims involved treaty violations and what many in Native communities considered to be the wrongful confiscation of their ancestral lands. Though it was only expected to last a decade, the three-member commission operated until September 1978, when the US Court of Federal Claims took control over any outstanding cases. During that time, nearly all of the federally recognized Native American nations filed at least one claim. Approximately 342 awards totaling more than $800 million were distributed. The individual judgments ranged from several hundred dollars to $31.2 million.[4] However, many Native Americans believed no monetary compensation would bring true justice to the situation. Critics felt the ICC simply forced Native Americans to monetize unfairly seized lands.

excess property. Since then, the government had been dragging its feet in coming up with a viable idea for what to do with the island and buildings. Members of the Sioux Club were sure this was exactly the opportunity the Native American community needed.

Spearheaded by Richard D. McKenzie, president of the American Indian Council, Allen Cottier, Martin Martinez, Garfield Spotted Elk, and Walter Means, a plot was hatched to peacefully invade and occupy Alcatraz Island. The five Sioux leaders and their followers would charter a tugboat and pack it with enough food and supplies to last for 30 days. After they landed, they would establish a control center from which they could state their demands to the government.

The First Occupation

On that breezy March afternoon in 1964, the Sioux Club's scheme almost worked. After Aylworth stepped aside, the five Sioux leaders trekked up the hill. McKenzie waved an American flag while Cottier read a statement he had written on deer hide parchment. "We'll be more fair to the government than they were to us," Cottier said. "We'll pay them forty-seven cents an acre, same as they paid California tribes when the government took their land."[5]

Walter Means and his son, 26-year-old Russell, hammered a beat-up mop handle into the ground to mark and claim their territory. Another Sioux leader, Tom

INFAMOUS ALCATRAZ

From the 1850s to 1963, San Francisco Bay housed one of the strictest and most terrifying maximum-security prisons in US history. Notorious criminals such as gangster Al "Scarface" Capone and murderer Robert "Birdman of Alcatraz" Stroud were locked up in cramped cells behind its walls. Nicknamed The Rock because of its steep jagged cliffs, the prison was a virtually escape-proof fortress. Many attempts were made during its years in operation, first as a military jail until 1933, then as a federal prison from 1934 to 1963. But no inmates are known to have successfully escaped. Due to expensive maintenance costs, the government shut down Alcatraz in 1963.

Brown, scrambled up a stone railing and flashed a tin tray in the air three times to signal success to anyone watching back on the mainland. The other Native Americans back near the boats whooped, hollered, and danced in unison.

But their euphoria was short-lived. While the group was busy celebrating, Aylworth had called his boss Richard Willard, the last acting warden of Alcatraz, at Willard's home in Concord, California. When Willard arrived on the island, he ordered the intruders to leave at once. "Fight it in court! Don't fight it out here!" he bellowed. "You got no right to trespass here. You're violating the law and I'm telling you, somebody's going to get [hurt]."[6]

RUSSELL MEANS

Russell Means was born on the Pine Ridge Sioux Reservation in South Dakota on November 10, 1939. His family moved to California when he was a young child. His brief trip to Alcatraz with his father in 1964 when he was 25 years old inspired Means to stay active in the Native American rights movement. In 1973, he and other leaders of a Minnesota-based group, the American Indian Movement (AIM), commanded a 71-day armed standoff with Federal Bureau of Investigation (FBI) agents and federal troops at Wounded Knee, a town where a massacre of Native Americans by US troops took place in 1890. The siege resulted in hundreds of arrests and the deaths of two protesters. In 1987, Means campaigned to become the Libertarian Party's candidate for the US presidency, but he lost to Ron Paul.

It's Over, for Now

After nearly four hours on the island, Leighton advised McKenzie and his crew to back down. Reluctantly they packed up their supplies, boarded the boats, and charted a course back to the mainland. As they neared the shore,

The March 1964 occupation did not last long, but it would be followed by more successful efforts to bring attention to Native American protests.

they saw a boatload of disgruntled federal marshals speeding toward the island in the other direction. The next morning, a headline in the *San Francisco Examiner* read "Wacky Invasion!"[7]

Nearly three weeks later, on March 27, McKenzie and the other Sioux leaders tried another approach. They filed a written petition with the government. In it, they stated their intentions to establish a university for Native American students on the island. But the government denied their petition. In July 1964, Alcatraz became the property of the General Services Administration (GSA), a federal agency tasked with, among other duties, managing government buildings and land.

The first takeover of Alcatraz had apparently failed. But it wouldn't be the last. Following the example of McKenzie and his crew, and emboldened by civil rights protests breaking out throughout the country, other Native Americans would soon take up the cause. Members of various tribes would try twice more to occupy Alcatraz. Their third attempt—on November 20, 1969— was the most successful and lasted more than 19 months.

As were many other periods in US history, the 1960s and 1970s were a time of great upheaval for Native Americans. Most were determined to set the record straight about the injustices that had befallen them for

Richard Oakes and others spearheaded a campaign that became a milestone in the history of Native American activism.

centuries. Although each one of them deserves credit, the key leaders of the Alcatraz movement included people such as Richard Oakes, John Trudell, and Stella Leach. Many of these people are not well known today. But without these hidden heroes, extraordinary change for Native Americans and the country as a whole might not have happened.

CHAPTER TWO

NATIVE HERITAGE

The first official endeavor by Native Americans to take over Alcatraz began on March 8, 1964. But the roots of what would become a near two-year occupation of the island in 1969 actually date back hundreds of years earlier. To comprehend why Native Americans were so starved for rights and recognition, it is important to first understand their complicated history.

Native Americans are the indigenous inhabitants of North, Central, and South America. Scientists have found evidence that more than 10,000 years ago, people from Asia migrated into North America. They crossed the Bering Strait, which at the time was a

Native Americans lived in the area that is now the United States for thousands of years before the arrival of large numbers of white people on the continent in the 1500s.

land bridge connecting the two continents. Until the Europeans began staking claims in the late 1400s, these Native Americans were the continent's only inhabitants.

Prior to the Europeans' arrival, most Native Americans were deeply connected to the wilderness and waterways. They formed thousands of tribes with independent governments and set up communities based on their religious beliefs and cultural traditions. Some, such as the Cherokee Nation in the southeastern United States, were primarily farmers and grew corn, beans, squash, tobacco, and sunflowers. Others, such as the Apache in the Southwest and the Sioux in the Great Plains of North and South Dakota, were nomadic hunters and herders, tracking bison and forging temporary camps across large swathes of territory. The Costanoans, coastal people later referred to as the Ohlone, settled mainly in the San Francisco Bay Area near Alcatraz Island. They fished abalone and mussels, and they wove intricate baskets out of willow, rush, and grasses from the surrounding region.

But beginning in the early 1500s and stretching well into the 1800s, the relationship between Native Americans and their environment changed. For one, invading Europeans from Spain, France, the Netherlands, and Great Britain sought to replace native spirituality with Christianity. The Europeans also laid permanent claim to millions of acres on North America's eastern seaboard. Consequently, either through peaceful negotiations and written treaties or by engaging in violent warfare, the land-hungry newcomers displaced hundreds of thousands of Native Americans from their homes.

Lacking immunity to common European ailments, many native people also died from infectious diseases carried to the Americas by settlers. Smallpox, malaria, measles, and yellow fever decimated their populations. Insufficient medical supplies and treatment, combined with the disruption of traditional food sources, led to many deaths

THE OHLONE

Native Americans have called the San Francisco Bay Area home for more than 10,000 years. The Ohlone were organized into 50 smaller tribes scattered around the region.[1] Known for their deep spirituality, these indigenous people cherished singing, dancing, and making crafts, tools, and boats from their natural environment.

In 1776, the Ohlone came into contact with Spanish settlers, who baptized them and forced them into missions. By 1810, disease had infiltrated their communities and they were forced to work hard labor and worship a Christian god.

As were many other tribes, the Ohlone were dropped from the list of federally recognized sovereign Native American nations in 1927. Today, they are still fighting to get their status reinstated. Tribes with this status are eligible for services from the US government.

Spanish soldiers were among those who invaded
Native American lands.

and had a severe negative effect on their traditional way
of life.

The Indian Removal Act

By the early 1800s, white settlers had begun pushing
further westward in search of more unclaimed land and
new opportunities. They petitioned the US government
to forcibly relocate eastern Native American tribes to
less desirable areas west of the Mississippi River, but
neither President Thomas Jefferson nor President James
Monroe took steps to ensure the moves happened.
Instead, Andrew Jackson, then a major general in the
US Army, led his own violent campaign to carry out the
task. From 1814 to 1824, he helped negotiate nine of
the eleven major land cession treaties to remove Native

Americans from their
homes, including taking
more than 20 million
acres (8 million ha) from
the Creek Indians—
approximately half of
present-day Alabama and
one-fifth of Georgia—in
the Battle of Horse Shoe
Bend.[2] In 1824, the Bureau
of Indian Affairs (BIA)
was established as a part
of the Department of War
to keep track of Native
American matters on newly
created reservations.

Then in 1830, after
Jackson was elected
president, Congress passed
the Indian Removal Act.
The law officially allowed
Jackson to grant land west of the Mississippi River to
Indian tribes that agreed to leave peacefully. In exchange,
the tribes were offered goods, financial relocation
assistance, and supposed unconditional protection by the

A QUESTION OF OWNERSHIP

Land-hungry European settlers drafted land treaties with Native Americans in exchange for money and supplies. But in the early years of European colonization, many Native Americans were unfamiliar with the Europeans' notion of land ownership. Many signed the treaties, thinking they could still use their traditional lands for hunting and grazing. When they violated the agreements, conflict broke out. Sometimes these wars raged for years. The Anglo-Powhatan Wars in Virginia (1609–1614, 1622–1632, 1644–1646), the Pequot War in Connecticut (1636–1637), and the Black Hawk War in Illinois (April–August 1832) were only three of the many conflicts that erupted between the colonists and Native Americans. Thousands of lives on both sides were lost.

US government. By the end of his presidency in 1837, Jackson had signed into law nearly 70 treaties with various tribes. As a result, as many as 50,000 Native American women and men migrated to what was then called Indian Territory, an area roughly the size of what is now Oklahoma.[3]

But though some tribes reluctantly relocated to new reservations to avoid violent clashes, others were not willing to abandon the land they had cherished for centuries. Some, including the Sioux in Montana and South Dakota and the Cherokee in northern Georgia and Tennessee, fought back. The Cherokee took the matter to court, too. In a landmark case pitting Cherokee missionary Reverend Samuel Worcester against the state of Georgia, the US Supreme Court decided in the Cherokee Nation's favor. But President Jackson ignored the ruling. In 1835, he negotiated the Treaty of New Echota, which traded all Cherokee land east of the

INDIAN TERRITORY

As part of the Indian Removal Act of 1830, Native Americans from the southeast were required to resettle in land west of the Mississippi River. The territory stretched from the Red River along northern Texas to the lower Missouri River along the northern border of present-day Nebraska. Tribes affected included the Cherokee, Creek, Seminole, Chickasaw, and Choctaw. Also affected were the tribes that already lived in the areas in which the US government forced people to resettle.

Mississippi River for $5 million.[4] Three years later, more than 17,000 Cherokee were rounded up and taken to Indian Territory in a journey often referred to as the Trail of Tears. Along the way, an estimated 4,000 Cherokee died from starvation and disease.[5]

Reservation Exiles

As the 1800s came to a close, most Eastern indigenous tribes were now sequestered either in temporary prison camps awaiting permanent placement or on reservations poorly maintained by the US government. Watched over by the BIA, they had few legal rights, were not considered US citizens, and had little say in their own governance. Most were forbidden to hunt or practice their spiritual traditions. Instead, they were taught the European way of life and forced to adopt the Christian doctrine.

One way this was accomplished was by implementing strict educational mandates. In 1879, US Army officer Richard H. Pratt founded the first government-funded school geared toward the so-called civilizing of Native American children. Similar to many of these boarding schools, the Carlisle Indian Industrial School in Carlisle, Pennsylvania, was located far from any reservation and aimed to strip its students of their customs and rituals so they could more easily assimilate into mainstream white culture. Boys were forced to wear military uniforms.

SIOUX LEADERS FIGHTING BACK

The late 1800s were a time of immense western expansion in the United States. During this period, the Lakota Sioux waged fierce battles to retain control of their land. Though the tribe was ultimately defeated, a few of its leaders stand out as heroes who fought valiantly for their cause.

From 1866 to 1868, a Sioux leader named Red Cloud orchestrated the most successful war effort against the United States by an Indian nation. He attacked a series of forts the US Army set up along the Bozeman Trail in the Bighorn Mountains of southern Montana. The skirmishes ended in the Treaty of Fort Laramie, which returned land that is now Western South Dakota, Montana, and Wyoming to the tribe.

But the terms of the treaty did not stick. Sioux leaders Crazy Horse and Sitting Bull took up the fight Red Cloud had started. In 1876, on the banks of the Little Bighorn River in southeastern Montana, the struggle culminated in a ferocious clash against a US cavalry unit led by General George Custer.

The Native Americans' triumph over Custer was short-lived, however. Another major incident between the Sioux and the US Army took place in 1890 at Wounded Knee Creek in South Dakota. There, US troops brutally murdered approximately 300 Sioux men, women, and children.[6] The massacre marked the beginning of the end of Native American resistance in the West.

In the decades after he led an armed struggle against the United States, Red Cloud led his people as they transitioned to life on reservations.

The Carlisle Indian Industrial School was in operation from 1879 until 1918.

Girls wore Victorian-style dresses. Supervision was strict and rules were enforced at all times. The schools forbade students from speaking their ancestors' languages.

The Dawes Act of 1887 was another tool whites used to suppress Native Americans. Also called the General Allotment Act, the Dawes Act broke up reservation lands into smaller parcels. Each head of a Native American household was given 160 acres (65 ha) to rent and farm until the family could prove it could grow enough food to sustain itself.[7] But many Native Americans weren't versed in the European methods of farming, and much of the land they were given was unsuitable for agriculture. White settlers soon took over many of the parcels. As a result, Native American landholdings fell from 138 million acres (55.8 million ha) in 1887 to 48 million acres (19.4 million ha) in 1934.[8]

By the 1900s, nearly two-thirds of reservation land in the United States had been taken from Native Americans and given to whites, often without compensation to the tribes.[9] Though the disastrous land-allotment policy was revoked under the Indian Reorganization Act of 1934, the damage had already been done. For Native Americans, the coming decades would be crucial in the fight to reclaim the land and dignity that was rightfully theirs.

> "Only by complete isolation of the Indian child from his savage antecedents can he be satisfactorily educated."[10]
>
> —John B. Riley, Indian school superintendent

CHAPTER THREE

SEEDS OF ACTIVISM

At the onset of the 1900s, life for Native Americans was far from ideal. North America's original inhabitants were not universally granted US citizenship at birth until 1924. Even then, many states, including Maine, Arizona, and New Mexico, denied them the right to vote in national elections.

According to the Meriam Report, a study commissioned by the US secretary of the interior in 1926 and published in 1928, the social and economic conditions inside the reservations were atrocious. Most communities were well below the poverty level and had little variety in nutritious food to eat. Overcrowding was common. Diseases

The lives of many Native Americans in the early 1900s were marked by poverty and discrimination.

such as tuberculosis and trachoma, an illness that causes blindness, ran rampant. Health-care facilities were few and far between.

On a national scale, Native Americans were once again faced with a seemingly insurmountable problem. The amount of money allotted to tribes had been reduced from $500 million to $12 million. Nearly 94 percent of those funds went to bolstering the BIA and keeping its programs running efficiently.[1]

To alleviate some of the suffering, the US government sought reform measures. On June 18, 1934, Congress enacted the Indian Reorganization Act, also called the Wheeler-Howard Act or the Indian New Deal. The law, proposed by Commissioner of Indian Affairs

John Collier and signed into law by President Franklin D. Roosevelt, prevented the future allotment of tribal lands to white individuals and returned much of the remaining extra land to the tribes. It also allowed for written constitutions, once again giving Native Americans the power to manage their own affairs. Finally, money was set aside for the establishment of a credit program for tribal land purchases and the formation of reservation-based day schools rather than boarding schools elsewhere.

As a result of the Indian Reorganization Act, 160 tribes adopted written constitutions from which to govern themselves.[3] Many set up their own businesses or took jobs in BIA offices to try to incite change from within. Large tracts of land were added to reservations. More than half of all Indian children were enrolled in public schools by 1950.[4] But despite these small victories, Native Americans had yet more obstacles to face. A new era of hardship was on the horizon.

"There is no reason why (the US government) should go on disgracing itself in Indian matters. President (Franklin Delano Roosevelt), Secretary Ickes, and the Indian Bureau have determined that the time has come to stop wronging the Indians and to rewrite the cruel and stupid laws that rob them and crush their family lives."[5]

–Commissioner of Indian Affairs John Collier, to a group of tribal leaders in South Dakota

Secretary of the Interior Harold Ickes, *seated*, finalized the first plan for Native American self-government following the passage of the Indian Reorganization Act.

Termination and Relocation

By 1953, some outspoken leaders in the US government had grown tired of giving federal assistance to tribes. Many wanted to do away with reservations and tribal self-governance altogether and thought it was time for Native Americans to fully integrate into mainstream white society without relying on government income. That year, Congress passed Public Law 280, which gave state governments the power to enforce criminal laws on reservations in Oregon, California, Minnesota, Nebraska, and Wisconsin. Congress's "termination" policy sought to make Native Americans on reservations subject to the same laws as the rest of the people in the United States. Under this policy, over the next 11 years, 109 tribes were terminated and lost official recognition by the US government. The government removed nearly 2.5 million acres (1 million ha) of land from protected status and sold it to whites. More than 12,000 Native Americans lost tribal affiliation.[6]

At the same time, the US government initiated a voluntary relocation program off the reservations to nine major cities: Chicago, Illinois; Denver, Colorado; Los Angeles, California; San Jose, California; Saint Louis, Missouri; Cincinnati, Ohio; Cleveland, Ohio; Dallas, Texas; and San Francisco, California. Participants were promised temporary housing and assistance in finding a job. They were also given start-up money depending on the number of children in the family. A couple with four children was supposed to receive $80 a week for up to four weeks.[7]

LAND ON THE CHEAP

In 1946, Congress created the ICC to settle tribal land disputes and arguments over broken treaties. Though Native Americans were compensated for their loss, the cash reward was based on the value of the land at the time it was taken. This was especially unsettling to a tribe in California. In 1959, the ICC awarded them $29 million for 64 million acres (26 million ha) stolen by whites in 1853. This works out to 47 cents per acre—a sum much less than what the land was worth.[8]

But as in the past, many of these government promises were not kept. In some situations, the assistance checks never arrived. In other cases, migrants couldn't find decent-paying jobs to match the hefty cost of rent, forcing them to live on the street. Still, between 1950 and 1980, an estimated 750,000 Native Americans migrated to urban areas in the Midwest and West in search of a better life.[9] A large portion moved to California.

San Francisco: A Hotbed of Indian Activism

The 1960s ushered in an era of activism and change in cities across the United States. San Francisco was at the heart of many protest movements. Heated debates and riots over the Vietnam War (1955–1975) were a constant occurrence. Activists preached the benefits of dropping out of mainstream corporate society and joining communes. Women marched in the street, demanding respect and equal pay in the workplace, and gay rights activists called for the implementation of antidiscrimination laws in all areas of society. African Americans sought to fight racism and achieve civil rights, following leaders including Dr. Martin Luther King Jr. and Malcolm X.

Amid this atmosphere of rallies and demonstrations against injustice, Native Americans organized their own activist groups, often around tribal ties. They founded the Sioux Club, the Navajo Club, the United Bay Area Council of American Indian Affairs, and the Intertribal Friendship House. They held powwows and celebratory dances, and they staged community meetings to discuss pressing issues such as the reclaiming of their ancestors' land. In 1961, a group of college-educated young people, Clyde Warrior, Karen Rickard, Mel Thom, Shirley Hill Witt, and Herb Blatchford, started the National Indian Youth Council (NIYC), the first independent Native American student activist organization in the United States. The group's mission called for Indian

PROTESTS AT SAN FRANCISCO STATE

In 1968, a major protest began at San Francisco State University. The Black Student Union and the student-run Third World Liberation Front organized a five-month campaign that began on November 6, 1968, and ended on March 20, 1969. African-American, Asian, Hispanic, and Native American faculty and students called for equal access to education for all; a more diverse curriculum that included multiracial and ethnic studies; and higher-level job openings for professors of color. As a result of the strike, the College of Ethnic Studies at San Francisco State was created in 1969. In the next decade, hundreds of other campuses followed suit. According to a 1981 report issued by the Education Resource Information Center, 439 colleges offered 8,805 ethnic studies courses by 1978.[10]

Mel Thom, *left*, and Herb Blatchford, *right*, were important figures in the NIYC.

self-determination, cultural preservation, and for the US government to uphold long-ignored treaty rights.

Perhaps one of the most outspoken figures in San Francisco at the time was LaNada Boyer, who relocated from the Shoshone-Bannock Fort Hall Reservation in Idaho to attend the University of California, Berkeley. In 1968, she and the director of American Indian Studies at Berkeley, Lehman Brightman, formed a student association they dubbed United Native Americans (UNA). The group attacked the BIA and published an intertribal militant newspaper, called *Warpath*. A quote from one particularly telling article summed up the prevailing attitude held by San Francisco's Native American community at the time:

> The 'Stoic, Silent Redman' of the past who turned the other cheek to white injustice is dead. (He died of frustration and heartbreak.) And in his place is an angry group of Indians who dare to speak up and voice their dissatisfaction at the world around them. Hate and despair have taken their toll and only action can quiet this smoldering anger that has fused this new Indian movement into being.[11]

Warrior, Rickard, Brightman, and Boyer were fed up with the way Native Americans had been ill treated for centuries.

WASHINGTON STATE FISH-INS

On March 2, 1964, inspired by sit-ins made popular during the civil rights movement, members of the NIYC staged their first large protest. They recruited actor Marlon Brando, Episcopal clergyman John Yaryan from San Francisco, and Puyallup tribal leader Bob Satiacum to fish for salmon in Washington's Puyallup River without permits.

Though Native Americans' right to fish in these waters was guaranteed by federal treaties signed in 1854 and 1855, state and local authorities wouldn't allow it. Protesters were arrested. The next day, nearly a thousand Native Americans, accompanied by Brando, marched to the capital building in Olympia, Washington. No agreement was reached. But thanks to the continued efforts of the NIYC during the next decade, the matter was finally settled. In 1974, a federal court ruled the tribes were entitled to half the salmon in western Washington. Plus, Native Americans were allowed to maintain their fishing rights and were guaranteed the right to regulate their own fisheries.

In the 1960s and 1970s, activists in San Francisco and throughout the nation made their voices heard.

For them and other many other Native Americans in the 1960s, the time for seemingly pointless talk and negotiation with the US government was over. A need for serious action had arrived. In the coming year, Boyer and others would take their activism to a whole new level. They would forge a path to take back their land once and for all.

CHAPTER FOUR

A STUDENT TAKEOVER

The summer of 1969 marked the six-year anniversary of the closing of Alcatraz federal prison. With the prison still standing but no one jailed inside, the government had yet to make a decision about what to do with the land. Should it become a museum? Should it be a tourist attraction? Should the building be torn down to make way for a park?

The city of San Francisco's Board of Supervisors had a few ideas. They were considering a proposal from Texas billionaire and ketchup fortune heir Lamar Hunt, who suggested turning Alcatraz into a theme park for the rich. There would be casinos and high-end restaurants, a space

After being emptied of its inmates in 1963, Alcatraz sat unused for several years.

exploration museum, and towering five-star hotels with manicured lawns. But the plan was so outlandish the people of San Francisco protested its implementation.

After Hunt's bid was dismissed, Native American activists—including San Francisco State student Richard Oakes and Berkeley student LaNada Boyer—cooked up a different idea. Using the brief 1964 occupation of Alcatraz as a model, they planned to retake the island. In September, a group of approximately 40 students met at Fisherman's Wharf in San Francisco Bay with their provisions and sleeping bags in hand.[1] The ferryboat they had arranged for transport to the island never appeared. But the seeds of a future takeover were firmly planted.

A Dangerous Spark

As the tail end of summer turned into autumn, San Francisco's Native American community grew increasingly anxious for action. But no one expected the

STATUES ON ALCATRAZ

There were many proposals for what to do with Alcatraz after it closed its doors as a prison in 1963. One San Francisco group, the United Nations Association, suggested building a memorial for peace. Another option was to build a shrine to Saint Francis, the Roman Catholic friar and preacher from the 1100s for whom the city was named. If the idea had been approved, the structure would have stood 300 feet (91 meters) high.[2]

catalyst for change would arrive in the form of fire. In the early morning of October 28, 1969, a four-alarm fire ripped through the San Francisco American Indian Center, destroying everything in its path. Before the blaze, the building had served tens of thousands of Native Americans throughout the Bay Area, providing health care, classes, legal services, cultural performances, and social programs. Though the origin of the fire was never discovered, one thing was certain: the city's Native American population was in desperate need of a new cultural center. For a few people in the Bay Area, Alcatraz seemed an ideal spot.

Unlike the 1964 Alcatraz takeover attempt, which was staged mostly by local Sioux Indians, a number of Native American groups with members from throughout the United States banded together to support a renewed effort. They called themselves the Indians of All Tribes. Richard Oakes, who was eager to try taking Alcatraz again after the failed attempt in September, volunteered to recruit more students and supplies.

The Indians of All Tribes drafted an official proclamation. It called for the development of a Center for Native American Studies. It also proposed an American Indian Spiritual Center, an ecology center, and a vocational training school for young people.

SAN FRANCISCO BAY AREA

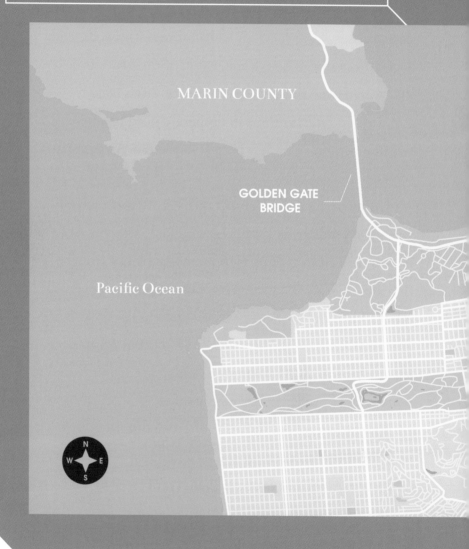

MARIN COUNTY

GOLDEN GATE
BRIDGE

Pacific Ocean

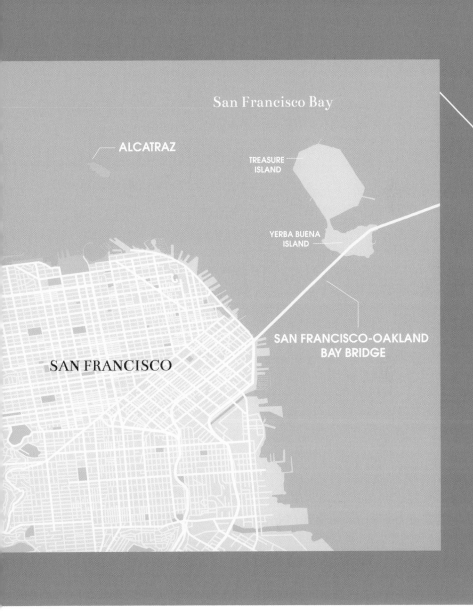

San Francisco Bay

ALCATRAZ

TREASURE ISLAND

YERBA BUENA ISLAND

SAN FRANCISCO-OAKLAND BAY BRIDGE

SAN FRANCISCO

It also laid out the terms of the agreement in a sarcastic tone. "We will purchase said Alcatraz Island for $24 in glass beads and red cloth, a precedent set by the white man's purchase of a similar island about 300 years ago," the agreement stated, in reference to the purchase of New York's Manhattan Island in the 1600s. "Our offer of $1.24 per acre is greater than the 47 [cents] per acre the white men are now paying the California Indians for their land."[3]

Finally, the group decided on an official date for the next occupation attempt: November 9. They invited members of the radio, television, and print media, including *San Francisco Chronicle* reporter Tim Findley, to cover the event. After the logistics were settled, all the Indians of All Tribes had to do was wait.

"We, the native Americans, re-claim the land known as Alcatraz Island in the name of all American Indians *by right of discovery*. . . . We will give to the inhabitants of this land a portion of that land for their own, to be held in trust by the American Indian Government—for as long as the sun shall rise and the rivers go down to the sea—to be administered by the Bureau of Caucasian Affairs (BCA). We will further guide the inhabitants in the proper way of living. We will offer them our religion, our education, our life-ways, in order to help them achieve our level of civilization and thus raise them and all their white brothers up from their savage and unhappy state."[4]

—*Indians of All Tribes proclamation*

A One-Night Protest

When Oakes and the other protesters arrived at Pier 39 on San Francisco's waterfront at 10:00 a.m. on November 9, they immediately realized the boats they hired had again failed to show up. To distract the press who were already there and waiting for something to happen, Oakes read aloud the Indians of All Tribes proclamation as the growing crowd of Native Americans danced around him and sang war songs. Meanwhile, Adam Nordwall approached a ship captain, Ronald Craig, and asked for his assistance. Craig agreed to take passengers aboard his three-masted ship, the *Monte Cristo*, but he made it clear he did not intend to land anywhere near Alcatraz. Instead, he would circle the island a couple of times.

Craig kept his promise. As soon as the *Monte Cristo* veered close to Alcatraz Island, it turned abruptly around to make another loop. But Oakes, a Hooper Bay Eskimo named Joe Bill, a Cherokee Berkeley student named Jim Vaughn, northern Californian Jerry Hatch, and Winnebago Ross Harden had other ideas. They dove off the side of Craig's boat and swam safely to shore. The soggy group was greeted by deputy warden and caretaker Glen Dodson, who refused to let them stay. Clad in waterlogged clothes, they boarded a boat and returned to the mainland 15 minutes later.[6]

Nordwall watched from the *Monte Cristo* as the boat passed by Alcatraz Island.

"We were supposed to get dressed up in all of their 'television costumes' and just make a pass around the island, to symbolically claim Alcatraz," Oakes told the press after the event. "But a lot of us were sick of doing things for the public; so when they sailed around the island, we decided to jump off the ship when it got close to Alcatraz, swim out to the island and claim it . . . by right of discovery."[7]

Despite Oakes and the others' bold actions, the media declared the event a failure. But they did not realize the efforts to take Alcatraz had only just begun. Later that evening, Nordwall arranged for a different boat—the *New*

ADAM NORDWALL

The son of a Swedish man and Chippewa woman, Adam Nordwall was born in 1929 on the Red Lake Indian Reservation in northwestern Minnesota. In 1935, his father died and his mother sent Adam and four of his siblings to Pipestone Indian Training School in Pipestone, Minnesota, where they were educated until 1945. Nordwall then met his future wife, Bobbie, a Shoshone Indian, at the Haskell Institute in Kansas. Later they moved to California and had three children.

Throughout his life, Nordwall was an outspoken advocate for Native Americans. In addition to his role in the Alcatraz occupation, he was the president of the Bay Area Council of American Indians and taught Native American Studies at California State at Hayward. However, some who were part of the Alcatraz occupation criticized Nordwall, who never spent a night on the island. They felt his accounts of the events were sometimes skewed and self-serving.

Vera II—to sneak back to Alcatraz. The skipper charged each of the 25 activists three dollars for the ride. Before the US Coast Guard could arrive and foil their plans, Nordwall and the rest of his crew set off from the dock. When *New Vera II* neared Alcatraz's shore, 14 occupiers jumped off before the boat's captain steered back toward the mainland, fearing trouble.

Nordwall did not make it onto Alcatraz that night. But Oakes, Vaughn, Harden, Bill, and Boyer leaped off the *New Vera II*. They spent the evening exploring some of the old cellblocks and trying to evade the authorities. The next morning, they surrendered to the Coast Guard, who informed them no one would be arrested for trespassing on federal property if they gave themselves up willingly. When they returned to dry land, the group of 14 started planning. They released a statement to the press. It read, in part:

> "On the island, you can hide just about anywhere, and no one can find you. And they would be so close sometimes, they'd be coming by so close, and it was almost like someone would be tickling you and you'd be trying to keep back your laughter because you didn't want to give yourself away. We felt like such kids."[8]
>
> —LaNada Boyer

Our people have suffered at the hands of the white man ever since we welcomed the Pilgrims to our shores. In

return for our help and kindness, the white man has stolen
our lands, killed our people and decimated our way of
life. . . . Now our young people cry out for social justice
and for an opportunity to reclaim their proud heritage.
The landing on Alcatraz Island is a symbol of our cultural
right to land and to life.[9]

In a week's time, they would finally be ready to set in motion a takeover that would be, if all went according to plan, bigger and better than ever before. It would be a pivotal event in the history of Native American activism.

As the activists left Alcatraz for the Coast Guard boats, they remained committed to their demands for social justice.

CHAPTER FIVE

THE OCCUPATION BEGINS

It was the early dawn hours of November 20, 1969. Oakes was ready. For the past ten days, he had crisscrossed the campuses of the Universities of California at Los Angeles and Santa Cruz, recruiting an estimated 90 students from the Indian studies programs for his cause.[1] He also informed Findley and members of the media of their latest plan.

Along with Boyer, Oakes and other protesters traveled by boats from Sausalito toward Alcatraz. As they neared the island, government and news media helicopters hovered overhead. The US Coast Guard

In November 1969, activists arrived on Alcatraz once again. This time, they intended to stay much longer.

attempted a blockade. But when Oakes and crewmembers boarded one of its vessels and threatened to take it captive, the Coast Guard relented. Oakes's boats were free to pass. When they reached the island, caretaker Dodson once again stepped out from his quarters to greet them, this time yelling, "Mayday, Mayday, the Indians have landed!" In a sly aside to Oakes, Dodson added, "I don't really mind [and] besides, I'm one-eighth Indian myself."[2]

After disembarking, the island's newest inhabitants immediately dispersed from the dock in case federal marshals sent by the GSA arrived to force an eviction. Some set up a temporary headquarters in what was once the prison warden's residence, while others went to explore the island's cell blocks and grounds to find places to sleep. They painted signs on the buildings' cement exteriors, proclaiming, "You Are Now on Indian Land," and "Peace and Freedom, Welcome, Home of the Free Indian Land."[3] Later that night, a spontaneous victory celebration erupted, with singing, traditional dancing, and drumming.

Tensions Build

The Native Americans' first full day on the island was thrilling but tenuous. There was no refrigeration, heat, or running water and very little electricity or working plumbing. The Coast Guard had established another

The activists quickly made it clear they considered the island Native American property.

blockade, so no supplies could come in or out. With all the media coverage, the occupiers were also unsure how the US government would react to the siege. National GSA head Robert Kunzig threatened to send in the police to forcefully intervene.

But President Richard Nixon was not prepared to take measures that might incite violence. He already had his hands full with other protests raging at the time, including protest rallies against US involvement in the Vietnam War and street riots in Chicago and Los Angeles regarding discrimination against African Americans. He knew if he gave the green light to expel the Native Americans from Alcatraz and the raid resulted in bloodshed, the troubles would only worsen.

Instead of federal intervention, Tom Hannon, a local GSA administrator who had successfully dealt with some of Alcatraz's occupiers during its two prior takeover attempts, took over negotiations. He chartered a fishing boat to the island and delivered a firm message to Oakes and his crew at 4:00 p.m.: Leave before noon on November 21 and none of you will be arrested.

The Alcatraz occupiers were not deterred. They quickly drafted a press release to members of the media, calling on them to elicit the public's support in financial donations and canned food:

The people of this country know a little of the real history and tragedy of the Indian people. What they do not know is the tragic story of the Indian people today. We intend to tell them that story. This is only the first stepping-stone of a great ladder of Indian progress.[4]

They also had a message delivered to William T. Devoranon, regional coordinator of the Department of the Interior in San Francisco. In it, they gave the US government a choice: to "use violence upon us as before to remove us from our Great Spirit's land, or to institute a real change in its dealing with the American Indian."[5]

Tensions were high. But the November 21 deadline came and went without incident. For the next three days, the Coast Guard blockade proved ineffectual, too. Though a

LIST OF DEMANDS

Despite the US government's apparent advantage and strength, the Alcatraz occupiers set their own negotiation terms. In their letter to Department of the Interior regional coordinator William T. Devoranon, they called for:

1. A face-to-face meeting with Walter Hickel, secretary of the Interior

2. A return of Alcatraz to Native American ownership within two weeks of Hickel's meeting

3. Enough financial backing to support the transformation of Alcatraz from a former prison to an Indian cultural complex—built, maintained, and run without any interference from any agency of US government

hot air balloon packed with supplies got blown too far off course to land, the occupiers were able to receive food, blankets, and other valuable resources such as toilet paper through other channels. One group of occupiers set off firebombs on one side of the island as a distraction. Using rope ladders, another group retrieved items from a fully stocked ship anchored adjacent to the steep cliffs on the island's other end. Finally, on November 24, the blockade was officially lifted.

Three days later, the Alcatraz crew celebrated their first Thanksgiving on the island. San Francisco's Bratskeller Restaurant volunteered to cater the affair and cooked up overflowing trays of mutton, venison, turkey, and corn. Lines snaked around the block on the mainland, with hundreds of supporters of all ages waiting to jump on board the boats and join in the Alcatraz celebration.

Getting Organized

With their stomachs full and government intervention at bay, it was time for Oakes and the rest of the Alcatraz occupiers to get down to business. The first item on their agenda was to set up the All Tribes Council of leaders that would make informed decisions about island affairs. The inaugural seven-person board, consisting of Oakes, Al Miller, Ross Harden, Bob Nelford, Dennis Turner, James Vaughn, and Ed Castillo, met as often as three times

daily in the beginning to
make sure everything was
running smoothly.

Next, Jerry Hatch was
put in charge of the island's
security. He appointed
sentries to monitor the
roof of the main cellblock
building and keep watch
on any suspicious activity
both on the island and in
San Francisco Bay. Licensed
nurse Stella Leach, who
was given a three-month
leave of absence from her
job at the Well Baby Clinic
in Oakland, established a
health clinic for residents,

WOMEN'S ROLES

In the 1960s and 1970s, many Native American societies did not have women serving in political leadership positions. Early in the Alcatraz occupation, it seemed as though this traditional reality would continue, with women taking care of much of the cooking, cleaning, and childrearing. However, women eventually entered leadership roles. Boyer became a leader in the Indians of All Tribes movement. In addition to running the health clinic, Leach also took a more active leadership role on the island after Oakes departed in early 1970.

with frequent visits from mainland doctors David Tepper, Robert Brennan, and Richard Fine. Maria Lavendar, Lou Trudell, and 22-year-old Dagmar Thorpe—granddaughter of famed two-time Olympic track-and-field gold medalist Jim Thorpe—took care of babies in a nursery. Back on the mainland, Joseph Morris helped establish the Alcatraz Relief Fund and converted an abandoned building on

Pier 40 into a warehouse for donations. By the end of the first week, the occupiers had received more than $4,000 in charitable goods and financial contributions.[6]

With money, supplies, and additional supporters sailing in daily and initial logistics taken care of, the Alcatraz council turned its eye to cultural development. On December 11, the Big Rock School opened in what had formerly been a movie theatre in Alcatraz's main cellblock. Run by 24-year-old Douglas Remington and 21-year-old Linda Aranaydo, the school taught reading and writing, math, geography, health, science, and Native American studies to 12 children living on the island in first through sixth grade. Earl Livermore resigned from his mainland job as director of the San Francisco Indian Center and set up an arts and crafts studio. While he and Francis Allen taught classes on beadwork, leatherwork, woodcarving, and costume decoration, Meade Chibatti and his wife, Noreen, taught dance and music and staged recitals for anyone interested in participating.

As 1969 wound down, the mood on Alcatraz was cautious but inspired. More supporters arrived on the island. Some stayed for the day, and others became permanent fixtures on the scene. Though there was still much left to do to further the cause of Indian self-determination, both residents and nonresidents began to adopt a more hopeful attitude toward the future. Perhaps this letter to President Nixon, written by Harold K. Dawson, a supporter of the occupation, best echoed what many people believed at the time:

> I think the Indians taking over Alcatraz is the most refreshing thing that has happened to this country in years, and certainly hope you will find a way to let them have it. Our treatment of the Indians has been one of the most shameful things in our history, and this is a glorious beginning to what could become something we could be proud of.[10]

CHAPTER SIX

A TURN FOR THE WORSE

The first few months of the Alcatraz occupation were an exhilarating time for Native Americans. On December 22, 1969, *Radio Free Alcatraz* began broadcasting from the island over KPFA-FM, a radio station in Berkeley. Hosted by John Trudell and using donated equipment, the 15-minute program ran locally on an irregular schedule and was distributed to stations in Los Angeles and New York. Each episode began with a recording of Native Canadian singer-songwriter Buffy Sainte-Marie's melodious rendition of the folk song "Now that the Buffalo's Gone." Trudell conducted interviews with residents, reported on national Native American affairs,

John Trudell later became a poet, musical artist, and film actor.

GRACE THORPE

Grace Thorpe was an essential component of the Alcatraz occupiers' public relations machine. The daughter of Jim Thorpe, she wrote press releases, answered letters from the public, and inspired celebrities such as actors Jane Fonda and Marlon Brando, actor and painter Anthony Quinn, and Native American singer-songwriter Buffy Sainte-Marie to visit. According to an interview she did with John Trudell on December 22, 1969, Thorpe spent her life savings to be a part of the Alcatraz occupation:

(It's) the catalyst and the most important event in the Indian movement to date . . . and certainly we need to have an organization that would foster our Indian heritage, as far as our history, our religion, our cultures. I can visualize here, an Indian village perhaps, I can visualize in my mind the entire area run by Indian people, and it could be an education thing for the entire world.[1]

and offered updates on the occupation as they occurred. Indian elders told stories passed down from members of their tribes.

To complement the efforts on the airwaves, Peter Blue Cloud created the *Indians of All Tribes Newsletter* in January 1970. In it, he printed top news items, original poetry selections, and general reports of goings on around Alcatraz. "Educating the general public to the Indian condition meant breaking out of official channels and into the public news media. The significance of *Radio Free Alcatraz* [and the *Indians of All Tribes Newsletter*] is revealed in this fact," remembered Steve Talbot, a non-Indian observer of the Alcatraz occupation. "For the first time Indian broadcasters reached people nationally on the critical issues in Indian affairs as the Indians saw them."[2]

News media unaffiliated with the Alcatraz residents continued to cover the occupation too, even after the initial excitement died down. Articles in the *San Francisco Chronicle* and the *San Francisco Examiner* provided lifelines to the outside world. They not only explained the Native Americans' reasons for taking over the island and the government's response, but also shed light on the evolving needs of the residents as supplies began to dwindle. Between November 20, 1969, and January 10, 1970, more than 125 articles on the occupation ran in these local papers.[3]

But despite the progress All Tribes members had made since setting foot on Alcatraz in late November, not everything on the island was as harmonious and organized as it appeared to outsiders. As early as mid-January 1970, cracks in the revolution had started to show.

Leadership Disputes

Beginning in January 1970, and continuing over the next 17 months, the conditions on Alcatraz Island became increasingly uncertain, both physically and psychologically. For one, the constitution of the community began to change. Members of the security force, who cheekily called themselves the Bureau of Caucasian Affairs, bought army fatigue jackets and started using violence to maintain order. Many of the peaceful, idealistic students who had joined the original protest movement left to attend to commitments elsewhere. Though some continued their daily commute by boat to their respective schools each day, most felt the trip back and forth from the mainland was getting to be too arduous and left the island altogether to return to their studies permanently. When the new school term arrived in January, most of the students originally at Alcatraz had left.

In the students' absence, a new group of protesters flocked to Alcatraz under different pretenses. Unlike the old guard's fight for equality and land rights for all Native Americans spearheaded by Oakes and Boyer, many newcomers were either non-Indian hippies who wanted to live off the land for free regardless of the reason, or more militant activists who viewed any negotiation with the government—and even between tribes—as a weakness. As reporter Findley wrote in the *San Francisco Chronicle* on January 7, 1970, "Like an ancient tragic curse come back to haunt them again and again, Indians on Alcatraz are apparently approaching a crisis in leadership that may

After many of the original activists left, the mood became less idealistic and the overall goals became less focused.

determine the future of their six-week-old occupation of the crumbling island."[4]

As the months stretched on, divisions within and among tribes grew wider. Protests against Oakes's leadership, as well as the All Tribes Council's decisions, happened more frequently. The leadership troubles finally came to a head in early January when Oakes's 13-year-old stepdaughter, Yvonne, fell from a third-story stairwell and died five days later on January 8. Suspecting that Yvonne's death was not an accident and was instead the result of jealousy over his disproportionate recognition in the press, Oakes and his family left the island for good.

Oakes's departure settled matters only slightly. To fill the gap in leadership, 50-year-old Leach stepped into Oakes's vacant role. Her sons followed her orders in helping to exercise leadership. But in the midst of infighting, excessive drinking and drug use—activities that were forbidden in the early days of the occupation—had become widespread. A new group of Vietnam War veterans and bikers called the Thunderbirds brought heroin, marijuana, and pills to the island. They also armed themselves with chains and pipes, and beat up anyone who opposed their behavior.

Crumbling Resources

A prolific drug problem, along with the lack of unity and informed consensus on major issues, meant circumstances on Alcatraz Island were worsening fast. Degrading infrastructure—deteriorating stairwells, broken cellblock locks, busted pipes—had become more of a safety concern. Most of the doctors who worked on the mainland had stopped visiting the island as often, and medical supplies began to run perilously low.

There were growing concerns about money, too. Excessive spending and the occasional misuse of public donations incited further friction within Alcatraz's leadership. By the spring of 1970, occupiers had spent an estimated $44,000 to keep the operation afloat. They needed $8 million to fix the water, electricity, and

The damaged and decaying buildings and infrastructure on the island made life difficult.

sanitation systems in most of the buildings.[5] They did not have such cash reserves.

Some residents, such as Eugene Cox, John D. Holloran, and James Robbins, resorted to desperate measures. They scavenged scrap metal from decaying bathroom fixtures and electrical wiring from some of the nonfunctioning buildings and sold it illegally to raise extra money. But the government found out and the men were promptly arrested. Cox, Holloran, and Robbins were later tried by the US District Court on February 25, 1972, and found guilty of selling nearly 1,700 pounds (771 kg) of copper for $600.[6]

Proposed Compromise

Despite the discord, the occupiers' original goal remained the same: full control of the island, the creation of a cultural center for Native Americans there, and enough money to keep everything running. But though members of the remaining All Tribes leadership committee tried to rectify some of the many problems, no one, including the federal government, seemed to be in a position to promote positive change. As a precautionary measure, the FBI sent in planes to take aerial photographs of Alcatraz. Although the government continued to insist on nonviolent negotiations with the Native Americans, it drafted a 17-step secret forced evacuation plan under the code name Operation Parks that called for helicopters, boats, and a brigade of police forces armed with guns and guard dogs, in case events got out of hand.

The government also came up with alternate paths to compromise, as meeting the occupiers' original demands was deemed financially unsound and logistically impossible. They asked more than two dozen mainland Native American groups representing 40,000 Indians from more than 78 tribes to form a new organization called the Bay Area Native American Council (BANAC).[7] In exchange, the federal government would donate $50,000 toward easing Native American joblessness

As the occupation stretched onward, the two sides were unable to find a workable compromise.

and poverty in the Bay Area and constructing a new San Francisco Indian Center. Though many BANAC members supported the proposal, the Alcatraz occupiers firmly rejected it.

Once BANAC was established, many who had been following the Native Americans' progress thought the Alcatraz issue was close to being resolved. But this was not the case. In fact, the introduction of the new mainland organization sparked further disputes. For one, Native Americans who lived on the mainland accused the Alcatraz occupiers of having tunnel vision and forgetting about the larger issues facing Native Americans as a whole. In return, mainlanders were blamed for abandoning a worthwhile cause and for giving in too easily to government demands regarding Alcatraz's fate. The gap between the two factions continued growing as the Alcatraz movement progressed.

Next, the government offered another option: to turn the island over to the National Park Service to create a revamped Golden Gate National Recreation Area. It would house a Native American museum and cultural center, feature monuments to honor fallen Native American heroes, and potentially carry a name taken from the Ohlone tribal language. In short, the island would be transformed from a once-shabby prison that housed hardened criminals to a hallowed place that paid tribute to Native Americans and their legacy.

Again, the Alcatraz occupiers refused the proposal. For them, land owned and run by anyone other than Native Americans was out of the question. In retaliation, in May the US government instructed the Coast Guard to haul away the barge that provided water to the occupiers for cooking, drinking, and washing. They also shut off the island's telephone service and electricity, including the power to the island's lighthouse and foghorn systems. The Alcatraz occupiers had reached an impasse. It would be a long summer ahead.

CHAPTER SEVEN

LEAVING ALCATRAZ

June 1, 1970, was a day to be remembered on Alcatraz. Despite the growing hardship and lack of supplies on the island, there was still plenty of reason to celebrate. Calling it Indian Liberation Day, the estimated 150 permanent residents at that time threw a huge party.[1] More than 800 visitors flocked to the island on free-of-charge fishing boats, carrying jugs of water for the residents.[2] Members of the crowd were affiliated with more than 100 tribes throughout the country. They danced, played music, sang, and feasted on stewed beef, corn, rice, and beans.

Bear Forgets, a 47-year-old Sioux Indian dressed in traditional garb, read aloud a

Bear Forgets, *left*, repeated the activists' position that Alcatraz was Native American land.

Declaration of the Return of Indian Land written on a piece of sheepskin. "We affirm that on behalf of all the Indian people or tribes from this day forward we shall exercise dominion and all rights of use and possession of Alcatraz Island," he yelled to the boisterous crowd.[3] Everyone cheered.

The merriment continued on into the evening. But at 11:05 p.m. on the mainland, GSA officer Thomas Scott received an alarming phone call from the US Coast Guard. It had just dispatched a boat to investigate a mysterious smoke plume emanating from Alcatraz Island. Another call came 15 minutes later, informing Scott the entire eastern end of the island appeared to be in flames. At 10:00 a.m. the next morning, the Coast Guard released an official statement: two of its boats had approached a group of occupiers on Alcatraz's docks to rescue them, but the Indians declined to evacuate. Three buildings, including the three-story warden's house and Alcatraz's lighthouse, were severely damaged in the blaze.

The June 1970 fire made the rough conditions on the island even worse.

The truth of what really happened that night has not been revealed. Some blame the increasingly militant Trudell and a few followers, who might have started the fires to get even with the government for removing the water barge and cutting the electricity. Others believe it was the government's doing, that it hired secret agents to scare the occupants into leaving. An article that ran in the *New York Times* claimed a gang of whites who had attended the Indian Liberation Day festivities had started the fires.

Whatever the truth might have been, one thing was certain: it seemed like the occupiers' days on Alcatraz were numbered.

Nixon's Message

After the fire and moving into the summer months, Alcatraz's residents had a much harder time surviving on the island. Many of the occupation's most ardent supporters left, including Leach. But as the occupation continued, President Nixon delivered a message expressing support for Native people, though the message was not directly connected to Alcatraz. On July 8, 1970, the president addressed the US Congress. In a speech that buoyed the spirits of many Native Americans, he said:

The first Americans—the Indians—are the most deprived
and most isolated minority group in our nation. On
virtually every scale of measurement—employment,
income, education, health—the conditions of the Indian
people ranks at the bottom. It is long past time that
the Indian policies of the Federal government began to
recognize and build upon the capacities and insights of the
Indian people.[6]

President Nixon's speech laid out the details of
a multifaceted plan that would formally end the
government's Indian termination program. It would
increase funding for education, health care, and economic
development on reservations and set aside money for
programs geared toward Native Americans in urban areas.
The plan also stipulated that some of the BIA-sponsored
programs on reservations would be run by Native
Americans instead of whites.

Finally, President Nixon proposed returning 48,000
acres (19,000 ha) of wilderness in northern New Mexico
to the Taos Indians.[7] Included in the deal was Taos Blue
Lake—an important spiritual site to the tribe. Nixon's
message was hopeful for Native Americans, but there
is no evidence he directly supported the protest actions
at Alcatraz.

Waning Support

Despite President Nixon's support for Native causes, the situation on Alcatraz was growing grim. The lack of foghorns and a working lighthouse in San Francisco Bay was becoming ever more dangerous for residents and mainlanders alike. Though the government offered to fix the problem, the occupiers refused to let the Coast Guard dock unless its ships brought fresh supplies of water. Instead, the government secretly hired two civilians who lived in high-rise apartment buildings in San Francisco to document any suspicious activity on the island.

By the end of the summer, conditions were abysmal. Food was rotting. Toilets were backed up. Alcatraz's population had diminished to approximately 40.[8] California governor Ronald Reagan had approved a

$50,000 grant, but the money was earmarked for programs for Native Americans in the urban areas of San Francisco and Oakland, not on Alcatraz.[10] Though Trudell and Boyer were still on board with the movement and active as ever, the atmosphere on the island was far from jubilant.

Still, on the one-year anniversary of the November landing, Trudell and Boyer released a press release in which they reiterated the occupiers' original goals. They also unveiled plans to build a $6 million college on the island called Thunderbird University, complete with a round ceremonial lodge and 96 wigwam structures that could house up to 300 future students.[11] Tuition would be free.

But on January 18, 1971, a catastrophe occurred. Because of the lack of foghorns and a working lighthouse, two oil tankers collided in the San Francisco Bay two

LEHMAN BRIGHTMAN IN THE BLACK HILLS

On August 24, 1970, members of the United Native Americans, led by Berkeley faculty member Lehman Brightman, a one-time Alcatraz occupier, traveled to Mount Rushmore in South Dakota to demonstrate for Lakota Sioux claims to the Black Hills. An estimated 30 protesters stood atop the monument while an additional 35—including some members of the Indians of All Tribes council—took the lower campground.[12] Each group faced off with armed police and US Park Service guards, but a peaceful end to the occupation was finally agreed upon. No one was arrested.

miles (3.2 km) west of Alcatraz. Nearly 800,000 gallons (3 million L) of crude oil gushed into the ocean.[13] Blaming the occupiers for the crash, public support for the Alcatraz movement dwindled even further.

On April 13, the government made one last attempt to negotiate with the occupiers by calling a closed-door meeting. US Attorney James Browning, Assistant Attorney General Harlington Wood, acting regional director of the GSA Bob Ireland, GSA special agent Larry Anderson, and other officials met with what was left of the All Tribes council. They asked if the occupiers would settle for land on the mainland to start a school instead of laying claim to Alcatraz. Trudell and the others firmly declined.

Forced Removal

For the government, the Alcatraz occupiers' adamant refusal to negotiate—again—was the last straw. Rather than wait for a new influx of supporters to inhabit the island during the summer, President Nixon's staff decided it was time to force the occupation to end. The order came down from John Ehrlichman, aide to the president, on June 11: "Go!"[14]

At 1:45 p.m., US marshals and FBI agents armed with guns, batons, and flashlights stormed Alcatraz Island. In less than 30 minutes, the remaining 15 occupiers—six

The final occupiers of Alcatraz were removed from the island and bused into San Francisco.

The government tore down several of the buildings on Alcatraz soon after the occupation ended.

men, four women, and five children—were taken into Coast Guard custody and escorted to the mainland. They were interviewed, given lunch, and provided with one night's stay at a hotel in San Francisco. No criminal charges were filed.

Oakes called the operation "a sissy victory."[15] In the months that followed, the government sent a cleanup crew to Alcatraz with bulldozers and a wrecking ball. They leveled some of the most corroded buildings, including the makeshift apartment complex where many of the occupants lived. A security team with guard dogs was set up around the island's perimeter to prevent further raids. After 19 months and 9 days, the Alcatraz occupation was officially over. But its far-reaching legacy had only begun.

CHAPTER EIGHT

THE OCCUPATION LIVES ON

The occupation of Alcatraz ended in June 1971. But Native American heroes such as Oakes, Trudell, and Boyer did not stop fighting for their cause. And neither the US government nor the rest of the world had stopped paying attention to their concerns. The same year the Alcatraz movement came to a close, 46 pieces of legislation that directly affected Native Americans were enacted. They included Public Law 92-265, which prolonged the ICC, and Public Law 92-189, which allowed for the creation of Navajo Community

Oakes, *left*, and other activists continued working to improve conditions for Native Americans throughout the country.

College, the first college in the country for and run by American Indians.

President Nixon also expanded the budget for the BIA by more than 200 percent in 1971. He established the Office of Indian Water Rights, which assisted Native Americans in ongoing water rights court cases; doubled the amount of money made available for Native Americans' health care; set aside $848,000 in scholarships for Native American students; and made it easier for Natives to address issues concerning the protection of their natural resources. The Office of Equal Opportunity tripled its spending on recovery programs for substance abuse on reservations.[1]

These changes in policy were groundbreaking for Native Americans who had previously been taken advantage of or ignored entirely. Before 1960, the federal court system balked at hearing most cases that concerned Indian affairs. In the 1970s, it presided over nearly three dozen such cases—triple the number from the decade prior. In 1978, one of the most significant legal victories occurred. The American Indian Religious Freedom Act ruled American Indian religions and religious ceremonies would be protected under the First Amendment to the US Constitution.

Alcatraz's Legacy

Despite the participants' failure to achieve their intended goals, the Alcatraz occupation was an important event in the history of Native activism. It inspired a new generation of heroes to demand change. During the next 40 years, America's first peoples engaged in continued protests, large and small, to reclaim the life, land, and liberty that were once theirs.

LEGAL MILESTONES

In 1990, Congress passed the Native American Language Act, which provided funding for programs that would help preserve traditional Native American languages in the United States. The Native American Graves Protection and Repatriation Act was also passed into law in 1990. This act mandates that federally funded museums, agencies, and educational organizations must return sacred artifacts and human remains to tribes. The actual process of returning these items is often controversial and contested.

By the 1970s, the Minnesota-based American Indian Movement (AIM) had become one of the most powerful and outspoken Indian activist groups in the United States. Led by 1964 Alcatraz occupier Russell Means and by cofounders Dennis Banks and Clyde Bellecourt, the group carried out the most visible and aggressive protest since Alcatraz in the weeks leading up to the November 1972 presidential election. More than 1,000 protesters from an estimated 250 tribes in 25 states traveled to Washington,

DC, to present a 20-point document to President Nixon.[2] In a demonstration they called the Trail of Broken Treaties, they took over BIA headquarters, kicked out the staff, and controlled the building for nearly a week. The protest ended peacefully, but not before AIM members removed or destroyed BIA documents and smashed windows.

In 1973, activists launched the most prominent Native American protest action of the 1900s. In February, approximately 200 members of AIM occupied Wounded Knee, South Dakota, the site of the infamous 1890 massacre of Native Americans. Federal officers besieged the small town and engaged in nightly firefights with the occupiers. During a siege lasting 71 days, gunfire killed two Native Americans and paralyzed an officer.[3] Hundreds of the activists were arrested. The siege finally came to a close in May after the AIM leaders negotiated a settlement. A judge later ordered their acquittal, finding that federal officers had manipulated witnesses in the case.

Six years later, AIM's work continued on an even larger scale. In 1978, powerful business lobbyists convinced the government to introduce 11 pieces of legislation. These bills were intended to eradicate Indian land and water rights in Maine and New York, as well as on reservations throughout the country; restrict fishing and hunting rights in Washington State; cancel treaties; close Native American schools and health-care facilities; and weaken tribal governments.

In protest and partly to pay homage to the Cherokee Trail of Tears in 1838 and the Long Walk of the Navajos in 1864, Dennis Banks and other AIM members organized an event they dubbed the Longest Walk. On February 11, 1978, demonstrators began in San Francisco and set out on a journey across the United States through blizzards and tornadoes to Washington, DC. Five months later, on July 15, 1978, they and more than 2,000 other supporters entered the capital for 12 days of rallies. As a result, none of the 11 bills were passed. In a press conference in Washington, DC, Alcatraz occupier Brightman remembered the historic event:

The siege at Wounded Knee was among the 1900s' most violent
confrontations between Native American activists and the
US government.

[We've] just completed one of the most courageous walks in this history of this country. . . . A lot of people said we never would make it. Officials at the Bureau of Indian Affairs bet we wouldn't make it, but we made it because we possess something that they didn't count on. . . . This walk, I'm extremely proud to be part of it.[4]

Today's Heroes

Today, the Native American journey toward reversing the wrongs of the past endures. Many people continue to be inspired by the efforts and hard-won successes of earlier generations. New activists are carrying on the work their ancestors started.

Harvard graduate Winona LaDuke, an Anishinaabe Indian, is a former Green Party vice-presidential candidate who ran alongside Ralph Nader in 1996 and 2000. She is an internationally acclaimed author, speaker, activist, and founder of Honor the Earth, an environmentally focused

DENNIS BANKS MARCHES FOR FREEDOM

Dennis Banks continued making protest walks in the 1990s. And 30 years after he participated in the first Longest Walk from California to Washington, DC, he made the same trip again. On February 11, 2008, he and thousands of followers traveled for five months from Alcatraz to the nation's capital to fight for the protection of Native American sacred sites, protest drilling on Navajo reservations, and support the building of more infrastructure such as schools and hospitals.

Native-led foundation that aims to improve communities using financial, technological, and social resources. In 1994, *Time* magazine named LaDuke one of the nation's 50 most promising leaders under the age of 40.

Institute of American Indian Arts professor Charlene Teters, a Spokane Nation Indian, jump-started what's now become a heated national debate regarding the use of Native American imagery and derogatory names in sports. Her activist career began in 1989 when she criticized the college she attended, the University of Illinois, for using a headdress-wearing Native American chief as its sports teams' mascot. She later became a founding board member of the National Coalition on Racism in Sports and the Media. Thanks to her and the group's efforts, the National Collegiate Athletic Association (NCAA) established strict guidelines in 2005 to help colleges discontinue the use of offensive ethnic team mascots. More than 200 US schools and universities have followed suit and stopped using racially offensive Native American names for their mascots.[5]

"When I first came to Harvard, I thought to myself, 'What kind of an Indian am I?' because I did not grow up on a reservation. But being an Indian is a combination of things. It's your blood. It's your spirituality. And it's fighting for the Indian people."[6]

—*Winona LaDuke*

The NFL's Washington Redskins are among the sports teams targeted by activists for using Native American names and imagery.

As for the island that inspired the occupation movement, the National Park Service officially took over Alcatraz in 1972. A year later, the island opened as a museum. Today, tourists can catch glimpses of the cellblocks, watch videos about some of the prisoners who were interned there, and see firsthand some of the graffiti left over from the 1969 takeover. They can also learn from exhibits detailing the occupation and the Bay Area Native community.

Alcatraz was not turned into a historic park to commemorate Native Americans, as the government had once promised. But each year in November,

Native Americans gather there to honor those heroes who dedicated more than a year of their lives to participate in the occupation. They honor those who are still fighting for the cause today. And they inspire new generations of activists to forge a more positive, equal-opportunity future.

In 2015, Boyer made one such voyage back to the island. It was the first time she had stepped foot on Alcatraz in 44 years. Along with old friends and newcomers, she participated in the Indigenous People's Sunrise Ceremony and reflected on the past. "I was there in 1969. I helped plan the whole take over," she said. "We must find inner strength to make our ancestors proud of us; it is because of all their sacrifice that we are alive today. It continues to this very day. We [still need] to stand up and resist. It still continues."[7]

The Occupation's Place in History

When American Indian activists boldly occupied Alcatraz Island for 19 months, they did so in the midst of a swiftly changing society and world. Those changes affected American Indians as much as any other group. By the late 1960s, many American Indian people, especially young people in cities, were frustrated by the lack of attention to their communities' needs. They were then, as American Indians are now, defined in large part by their invisibility

In the years since the occupation, a variety of Native American groups have returned to commemorate the past and continue fighting for their communities.

as contemporary people with real needs and real lives. Protest and other forms of political action had been on the increase throughout the decade, but Alcatraz provided an opportunity to carry their message to a wider audience.

The San Francisco Bay Area was not at the center of the world of American Indian activism, but the Alcatraz occupiers built a movement there that inspired many later activists. The 19-month occupation was impractical, dangerous, and difficult. But those who proclaimed "We hold the Rock!" were deeply committed to staying on the island until their demand to turn the island into a

Evidence of the occupation of Alcatraz is still clearly visible to tourists today.

cultural center was met. Life on the island represented freedom and prompted tremendous political creativity. At times it also featured lawlessness, violence, chaos, and extreme boredom. All the built-in contradictions of the American Indian world were present in the occupation. Gaps existed between Native Americans in cities and those on reservations, as well as between those with educational opportunities and those stuck in poverty. Some were committed to radical political action, whereas others worked within the federal governmental system to improve Native lives. The occupation of Alcatraz ended unceremoniously, with 15 people being taken off the island by federal officers. However, the symbolism of bold protest that could overcome invisibility would live on.

TIMELINE

1824

The US Congress creates the Bureau of Indian Affairs in the Department of War to oversee day-to-day affairs of Native Americans on reservations.

1830

Congress passes the Indian Removal Act, authorizing the relocation of Native Americans from throughout the eastern United States to west of the Mississippi River.

1838

The US Army rounds up nearly 17,000 Cherokee from Georgia and transports them to Indian Territory in what is now called the Trail of Tears. Approximately 4,000 Native Americans die along the way.

1868

The US government and the Lakota Sioux sign the Treaty of Fort Laramie, ending Red Cloud's two-year war in Montana.

1876

The Sioux, Cheyenne, and Arapaho tribes defeat General George Custer at the Battle of Little Bighorn in Montana. The event is later called Custer's Last Stand.

1887

Congress passes the Dawes Act (also called the General Allotment Act), which authorizes the breaking up of Native American land into individual parcels.

1924

Native Americans become recognized as US citizens at birth.

1934

Congress passes the Indian Reorganization Act to improve reservation conditions for Native Americans; Alcatraz Island becomes a federal prison.

1946

The Indian Claims Commission (ICC) is created to discuss and settle disputes between the US government and Native American tribes over the illegal seizure of Native lands.

1953

The US government starts a "termination program," ending federal involvement with all tribal groups.

1963

Alcatraz prison closes.

1964

Members of the San Francisco Sioux Club stage their first mini-invasion of Alcatraz Island on March 8.

1969

On October 28, the San Francisco American Indian Center burns down; on November 20, the nearly two-year occupation of Alcatraz begins.

1970

In May, electricity, water, and telephone service are shut off on Alcatraz Island; fires destroy the warden's house in June; President Nixon announces an end to the termination program.

1971

The US government removes the remaining occupiers from Alcatraz Island in June.

1972

The National Park Service takes control of Alcatraz Island; Richard Oakes is killed during a dispute at a camp in northern California.

1978

The American Indian Religious Freedom Act passes.

1990

The Native American Language Act and the Native American Graves Protection and Repatriation Act are passed.

ESSENTIAL FACTS

KEY FIGURES

- A Shoshone-Bannock Indian, LaNada Boyer founded the radical group United Native Americans. Boyer was a part of the November 9, 1969, raid on Alcatraz and became an integral leader during the November 20 occupation.

- A Chippewa Indian, Adam Nordwall was one of the founders of the United Bay Area Council in 1961. Nordwall took part in the 1964 invasion of Alcatraz and chaired BANAC during the November 20 occupation.

- A Mohawk Indian, Richard Oakes was a principal organizer of the November 9 and November 20, 1969, Alcatraz invasions and became an unofficial spokesperson for the occupations.

- A Santee Sioux Indian, John Trudell pioneered the *Radio Free Alcatraz* radio program, became an Indians of All Tribes leader in 1970, and served as AIM chairman after the Occupy Alcatraz movement ended.

KEY ORGANIZATIONS

- Founded in 1968, the American Indian Movement's objectives include the sovereignty of Native American lands and peoples, preservation of their ancient traditions, and enforcement of all treaties made with the US government.

- The Bay Area Native American Council was created by Adam Nordwall and others to address the needs of dozens of mainland Native American groups in the San Francisco Bay Area during the late 1960s and 1970s.

- Part of the US Department of the Interior, the Bureau of Indian Affairs manages federal programs designed to benefit the Native American people and administers Native American land held in trust by the government.

- Founded in 1961, the National Indian Youth Council was the first independent Native American youth organization in the US and used radical tactics to fight for tribal sovereignty and the elimination of the BIA.

IMPACT ON SOCIETY

According to some members of the press and those critical of the movement at the time, the Native American occupation of Alcatraz in 1969 wasn't a successful demonstration. The government didn't turn the island over to the Native American community, nor were the occupiers permitted to create a permanent cultural center and school to honor their rich heritage and culture. But heroes such as Richard Oakes, Adam Nordwall, LaNada Boyer, Grace Thorpe, and John Trudell accomplished something more. They provided a spark for other Native American civil rights protests of the era and inspired future generations of American Indians to fight for self-determination and reclaim the land that was once theirs.

QUOTE

"Now our young people cry out for social justice and for an opportunity to reclaim their proud heritage. The landing on Alcatraz Island is a symbol of our cultural right to land and to life."

—Alcatraz occupiers, 1969

GLOSSARY

ASSIMILATE
Blend in; resemble or liken.

ATROCIOUS
Awful; extremely unpleasant.

BLOCKADE
The act of isolating or closing off a place to prevent people or goods from entering or leaving.

CONFISCATION
The act of taking away or seizing someone's property.

DISCRIMINATION
Unfair treatment of other people, usually because of race, age, or gender.

HEADDRESS
A decorative covering for the head, especially one worn on ceremonial occasions.

INDIGENOUS
Originating in or native to a place.

MISSIONARY
A church employee who is sent to another country to teach others about the church or to operate a school or hospital.

NOMADIC
Moving from one place to another.

NOTORIOUS
Infamous; known for a bad reason.

RESERVATION
Land set aside for a Native American tribe, often smaller than their traditional lands.

SELF-DETERMINATION
The process by which a person or group governs themselves.

SEQUESTERED
Isolated from.

SOVEREIGNTY
The power of a state or group to govern itself.

ADDITIONAL RESOURCES

SELECTED BIBLIOGRAPHY

Eagle, Adam Fortunate, and Tim Findley. *Heart of the Rock: The Indian Invasion of Alcatraz*. Norman, OK: U of Oklahoma P, 2002. Print.

Johnson, Troy R. *The Occupation of Alcatraz Island*. Urbana, IL: U of Illinois P, 1996. Print.

Smith, Paul Chaat, and Robert Warrior. *Like a Hurricane: The Indian Movement from Alcatraz to Wounded Knee*. New York: New Press, 1996. Print.

FURTHER READINGS

Murphy, Claire Rudolf. *The Children of Alcatraz: Growing Up on the Rock*. New York: Walker Children's Publishing, 2006. Print.

Treuer, Anton. *Atlas of Indian Nations*. Washington, DC: National Geographic, 2014. Print.

Vander Hook, Sue. *Trail of Tears*. Minneapolis, MN: Abdo, 2010. Print.

Watson, Stephanie. *The Escape from Alcatraz*. Minneapolis, MN: Abdo, 2012. Print.

WEBSITES

To learn more about Hidden Heroes, visit **booklinks.abdopublishing.com**. These links are routinely monitored and updated to provide the most current information available.

FOR MORE INFORMATION

For more information on this subject, contact or visit the following organizations:

ALCATRAZ ISLAND

Golden Gate National Recreation Area
San Francisco, CA 94122
415-561-4900
https://www.nps.gov/alca/index.htm
Visitors to Alcatraz can explore the island where the infamous decommissioned prison still stands. Through hands-on visual and audio exhibits, they can learn about the nearly two-year Native American occupation of 1969 and feel what it is like to be locked inside a jail cell.

NATIONAL MUSEUM OF THE AMERICAN INDIAN

The National Mall
Fourth Street & Independence Avenue Southwest
Washington, DC 20560
202-633-1000
http://www.nmai.si.edu
The National Museum of the American Indian houses one of the world's largest and most diverse collections of Native American artifacts, including clothing, pottery and woven baskets, and archeological finds. The museum's building, landscaping, and wide range of exhibitions were all designed in collaboration with more than 1,200 tribes and communities from throughout the Americas.

SOURCE NOTES

CHAPTER 1. AN ATTEMPTED INVASION

1. Adam Fortunate Eagle and Tim Findley. *Heart of the Rock*. Norman, OK: U of Oklahoma P, 2002. Print. 7–12.

2. Ibid.

3. Ibid.

4. Paul C. Rosier. "Indian Claims Commission." *Dictionary of American History*. Gale Group Inc., 2003. Web. 7 June 2016.

5. Adam Fortunate Eagle and Tim Findley. *Heart of the Rock*. Norman, OK: U of Oklahoma P, 2002. Print. 7–12.

6. Ibid.

7. Ibid.

CHAPTER 2. NATIVE HERITAGE

1. "Ohlones and Coast Miwoks." *Golden Gate National Recreation Area*. National Park Service, n.d. Web. 31 Aug. 2016.

2. "Indian Treaties and the Removal Act of 1830." *Bureau of Public Affairs*. US Department of State, n.d. Web. 7 June 2016.

3. Ibid.

4. Ibid.

5. "A Brief History of the Trail of Tears." *Cherokee.org*. Cherokee Nation, n.d. Web. 7 June 2016.

6. "Wounded Knee Massacre." *Encyclopedia of the Great Plains*. University of Nebraska–Lincoln, 2011. Web. 31 Aug. 2016.

7. "Archives of the West: The Dawes Act, February 8, 1887." *PBS.org*. Oregon Public Broadcasting, 2001. Web. 7 June 2016.

8. "History of Allotment." *Indian Land Tenure Foundation*. ITLF, 2016. Web. 31 Aug. 2016.

9. "An Introduction to Indian Nations in the United States." *NCAI.org*. NCAI, n.d. Web. 7 June 2016.

10. Charla Bear. "American Indian Boarding Schools Haunt Many." *Morning Edition*. NPR, 12 May 2008. Web. 7 June 2016.

CHAPTER 3. SEEDS OF ACTIVISM

1. "A Bill of Rights for Indians." *History Matters*. History Matters, n.d. Web. 31 Aug. 2016.

2. *The Meriam Report (1928) Investigates Failed US Indian Policy*. Baltimore, MD: Johns Hopkins P, 1928. Print.

3. "Indian Reorganization Act." *Encyclopædia Britannica*. Encyclopædia Britannica, 2016. Web. 7 June 2016.

4. Ibid.

5. "A Bill of Rights for Indians." *History Matters*. History Matters, n.d. Web. 31 Aug. 2016.

6. "Termination Policy, 1953–1968." *NRCPrograms.org*. American Indian Relief Council, n.d. Web. 7 June 2016.

7. "The Urban Relocation Program." *Indian Country Diaries*. NAPT, 2006. Web. 7 June 2016.

8. Joanne Barker. *Native Acts: Law, Recognition, and Cultural Authenticity*. Raleigh, NC: Duke UP, 2011. Print. 151–152.

9. "The Urban Relocation Program." *Indian Country Diaries*. NAPT, 2006. Web. 7 June 2016.

10. Denize Springer. "Campus Commemorates 1968 Student-Led Strike." *SFSU.edu*, SFSU, 22 Sept. 2008. Web. 7 June 2016.

11. Troy Johnson. *Contemporary Native American Political Issues*. Lanham, MD: Rowman Altamira, 2000. Print. 295.

CHAPTER 4. A STUDENT TAKEOVER

1. Troy Johnson. *The Occupation of Alcatraz Island*. Urbana, IL: U of Illinois P, 1996. Print. 51–53.

2. "Schemes and Dreams." *AlcatrazHistory.com*. Ocean View Publishing, n.d. Web. 7 June 2016.

3. Troy Johnson. *The Occupation of Alcatraz Island*. Urbana, IL: U of Illinois P, 1996. Print. 54.

4. Ibid. 56–57.

5. Carl Nolte. "Timothy D. Findley—Investigative Reporter—Dies." *SF Gate*. Heart Communications, 24 Dec. 2010. Web. 7 June 2016.

SOURCE NOTES
CONTINUED

6. Troy Johnson. *The Occupation of Alcatraz Island*. Urbana, IL: U of Illinois P, 1996. Print. 56–58.

7. Ibid. 58.

8. Adam Fortunate Eagle and Tim Findley. *Heart of the Rock*. Norman, OK: U of Oklahoma P, 2002. Print. 83.

9. Troy Johnson. *The Occupation of Alcatraz Island*. Urbana, IL: U of Illinois P, 1996. Print. 63.

CHAPTER 5. THE OCCUPATION BEGINS

1. Troy Johnson. *The Occupation of Alcatraz Island*. Urbana, IL: U of Illinois P, 1996. Print. 66.

2. Ibid. 65–67.

3. Ibid. 67.

4. Ibid. 68.

5. Ibid. 69–70.

6. Ibid. 80.

7. Ibid. 81.

8. Ibid. 85.

9. Ibid. 80–81.

10. Ibid. 92, 245.

CHAPTER 6. A TURN FOR THE WORSE

1. Troy Johnson. *The Occupation of Alcatraz Island*. Urbana, IL: U of Illinois P, 1996. Print. 108.

2. Ibid. 86.

3. Ibid. 93.

4. Ibid. 154.

5. Ibid. 160.

6. Ibid.

7. Ibid. 188.

CHAPTER 7. LEAVING ALCATRAZ

1. "Many Visitors Carry Water to Alcatraz Indian." *Desert Sun.*
Gannett Company, 1 June 1970. Web. 7 June 2016.

2. Ibid.

3. Ibid.

4. Ibid.

5. Troy Johnson. *The Occupation of Alcatraz Island.* Urbana, IL:
U of Illinois P, 1996. Print. 226.

6. Ibid. 197–198.

7. Ibid. 198.

8. Ibid. 202.

9. Ibid. 218.

10. Ibid. 201.

11. Ibid. 208.

12. Ibid. 227.

13. Ibid. 208.

14. Ibid. 213.

15. Ibid.

CHAPTER 8. THE OCCUPATION LIVES ON

1. Troy Johnson. *The Occupation of Alcatraz Island.* Urbana, IL:
U of Illinois P, 1996. Print. 218.

2. "The Trail of Broken Treaties." *AIMMovement.org.* American
Indian Movement, 31 Oct. 1972. Web. 7 June 2016.

3. "Wounded Knee." *History.* History, n.d. Web. 31 Aug. 2016.

4. Quanah Brightman. "Dr. Lehman Brightman Led the Longest
Walk 1978." *YouTube.* YouTube, 30 July 2010. Web. 7 June 2016.

5. "Change the Mascot Fact Sheet." *Change the Mascot.*
Change the Mascot, 2016. Web. 31 Aug. 2016.

6. Jennifer H. Arlen. "Winona LaDuke: Education of a Fighter."
Harvard Crimson. Harvard, 10 Nov. 1980. Web. 31 Aug. 2016.

7. Katrina Socco. "First Return to Alcatraz in 44 Years."
OccupyWallStreet. OccupyWallStreet, n.d. Web. 7 June 2016.

INDEX

ABOUT THE
AUTHOR

Alexis Burling has written dozens of articles and books for young readers on a variety of topics including current events and famous people, nutrition and fitness, careers and money management, and relationships and cooking. She is also a book critic with reviews of both adult and young adult books, author interviews, and other industry-related articles published in the *New York Times*, the *Washington Post*, the *San Francisco Chronicle*, and more. Alexis visited Alcatraz Island with her family when she was a child. She vividly remembers the thrilling tour, which described the 1969 takeover and its effect on history.